THE LUISEÑO

NORA ELLISON

PowerKiDS
press™

New York

Published in 2018 by The Rosen Publishing Group, Inc.
29 East 21st Street, New York, NY 10010

Editor: Melissa Raé Shofner
Book Design: Michael Flynn
Interior Layout: Rachel Rising

Photo Credits: Cover Nancy Carter/North Wind Picture Archives/Alamy Stock Photo; p.4 Culture Club/Hulton Archive/ Getty Images; p. 5 Olinchuk/Shutterstock.com; p.7 Jeffrey B. Banke/Shutterstock.com; p. 9 Shannon Switzer/National Geographic Magazines/Getty Images; p. 11 Witold Skrypczak/Lonely Planet Images/Getty Images; p. 13 https://commons.wikimedia.org/wiki/File:Luiseno_drawing_early_1800s.jpg; p. 15 Courtesy of the Library of Congress; p. 16 Robert Chao/Shutterstock.com; p. 17 NaturesMomentsuk/Shutterstock.com; p. 19 Sherry V Smith/ Shutterstock.com; p. 20 Courtesy of the UCLA Library; p. 21 Kevin Key/Shutterstock.com; p. 23 Hulton Archive/ Hulton Archive/Getty Images; p. 24 Byron W.Moore/Shutterstock.com; p. 25 LagunaticPhoto/Shutterstock.com; p. 27 iStockphoto.com/ YangYin; p. 29 George Rinhart/Corbis Historical/Getty Images.

Cataloging-in-Publication Data

Names: Ellison, Nora.
Title: The Luiseño / Nora Ellison.
Description: New York : PowerKids Press, 2018. | Series: Spotlight on the American indians of California | Includes index.
Identifiers: ISBN 9781538324646 (pbk.) | ISBN 9781538324615 (library bound) | ISBN 9781538324653 (6 pack)
o Indians--Juvenile literature. | Indians of North America--California.
Classification: LCC E99.L9 E55 2018 | DDC 979.4004'9745--dc23

Manufactured in China

CPSIA Compliance Information: Batch #BW18PK For further information contact Rosen Publishing, New York, New York at 1-800-237-9932.

CONTENTS

CHAPTER ONE

THE EARLY LUISEÑOS

Around 2,000 years ago, **ancestors** of the Luiseño Indians set up villages along the southern coast of present-day California. These American Indians occupied lands that stretched from Santiago Peak in the north to Agua Hedondo Creek in the south. Their home region continued into the interior of California to the valleys of the coastal mountains.

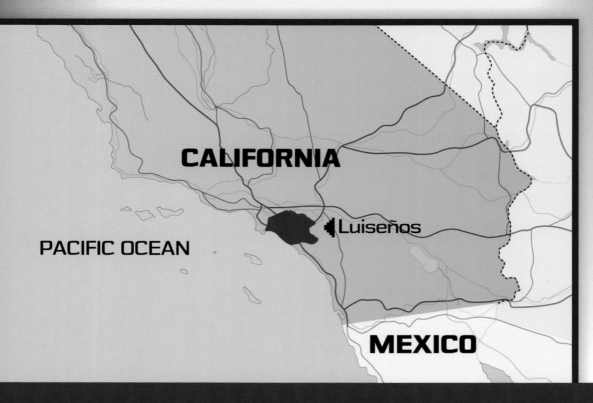

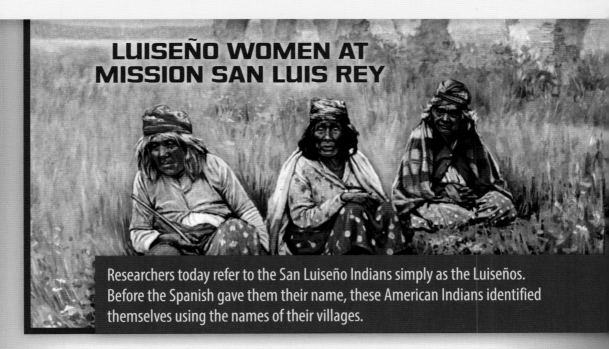

LUISEÑO WOMEN AT MISSION SAN LUIS REY

Researchers today refer to the San Luiseño Indians simply as the Luiseños. Before the Spanish gave them their name, these American Indians identified themselves using the names of their villages.

By 1400, these American Indians had created the communities that were discovered by European explorers. In 1798, the Spanish established Mission San Luis Rey in Southern California. The Spanish settlers gave the American Indians the name "San Luiseños" because many of them lived at the mission.

Mission San Luis Rey was a great success. However, after it was shut down, the Luiseños faced more than a century of **discrimination** and hatred. Even with these challenges, the Luiseños have endured. Today, they're recognized as one of the most remarkable American Indian groups in California.

CHAPTER TWO

VILLAGE LIFE

When Spanish colonists arrived in California in 1769, there were likely around 50 Luiseño villages in the area. There were between 50 and 500 people living in each village. The Luiseños always built their villages near a water source, such as a river or creek. The largest villages were found along the coast.

Luiseño families lived in cone-shaped huts built around a large, open space. These huts may have been made out of bark, brush, or reeds and were built inside shallow pits about 2 feet (0.6 m) deep. In the middle of each hut was a small fire pit. An opening in the roof allowed smoke out and sunlight in. Based on the settlements of other California American Indians, researchers believe most Luiseño villages also had a larger home where the chief lived.

Luiseño Indians living in the mountains would sometimes make their houses out of cedar bark. Willow branches were another popular building material for Luiseño homes.

There was at least one sweat lodge in each Luiseño village. Sweat lodges were used for religious cleansing and healing. They were similar to the huts in which the Luiseños lived, but the pits in which they were built were slightly deeper. Inside each sweat lodge, a fire produced strong heat. Smoke from the fire slowly escaped through a small hole in the roof. Thick layers of mud covered the inside and outside of the walls to keep the heat in.

After spending time in a sweat lodge, the Luiseños used deer ribs or curved sticks to scrape away their sweat. Many people followed their visit to the sweat lodge with a swim in a nearby creek or river.

The Luiseños also set up various kinds of rectangular pole-and-brush coverings for shade. Both men and women sat under these structures to avoid the hot California sun while they worked.

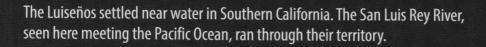

The Luiseños settled near water in Southern California. The San Luis Rey River, seen here meeting the Pacific Ocean, ran through their territory.

9

CHAPTER THREE

FOOD AND DRINK

The Luiseños ate many foods, including seeds, nuts, insects, fruits, vegetables, eggs, shellfish, and fish. They also ate meat from deer, elk, and small animals such as rabbits. Berries were crushed to make drinks. Other plants were boiled to produce a kind of tea.

The Luiseños used several cooking methods. When the weather allowed, they prepared their meals outside. Some foods were roasted over an open flame. Other items were smoked using slow-burning fires. Some meals were prepared using steam.

The Luiseños used pottery, stone bowls, and tightly woven baskets to prepare their meals. Before cooking, some foods were wrapped in leaves or clay. The Luiseños also knew how to preserve food for later use. Fruits and vegetables that weren't eaten immediately were dried in the sun. Fish and meat could be salted and smoked.

The Luiseños used special stones called pestles, mortars, manos, and metates to crush foods such as nuts and seeds.

CHAPTER FOUR

ARTS, CRAFTS, AND GAMES

The Luiseños were excellent artists and craftspeople. As with most other early American Indians, stone was one of their most important resources. They used stone to make bowls, beads, arrowheads, spear points, smoking pipes, and many other useful objects.

The Luiseños were also expert pottery makers. They used clay from nearby streambeds and hillsides to make beads, bowls, plates, and jars, among other things. Some pottery makers decorated their creations with paintings or carvings.

Many **minerals** were transformed into useful materials. Naturally occurring tar was collected from the beaches and used as a kind of glue. Carbon was used to make black paint.

The Luiseños used parts of the animals they hunted to make useful items. Bones, feathers, claws, hides, and shells were used to make many things, including clothing, toys, and tools.

This drawing shows two Luiseño men holding rattles and wearing clothing made of string and feathers. Pablo Tac, the artist, was a Luiseño man who lived at Mission San Luis Rey in the 1820s and 1830s.

Luiseño women and girls collected various types of plants and wove them into many things, including bowls, hats, and jars. Their baskets were decorated with tan, black, or brown designs. The Luiseños also used plants to make things such as rope, shoes, and nets for hunting and fishing. Dried gourds were made into rattles. Wood and plant stems, called cane, were popular materials for tools such as clubs and digging sticks. They were also used to make arrows, canoe paddles, fish traps, musical instruments, poles, spears, and many other tools.

The Luiseños also used wood and cane to make balls for sports. Some of the games they played were similar to modern sports such as hockey. Some Luiseño villages had a large, flat, open area that was set aside for sports contests. Whenever they gathered in large groups, people often found time to play games together.

Maria Antonia, a Luiseño woman, is seen here weaving a basket in the early 1900s. She lived in the Luiseño village of Pala.

CHAPTER FIVE

THE SHAPE OF SOCIETY

The Luiseños had a **complex** social structure. Individuals were assigned to a group based on age, birthplace, gender, their father's social status, and how much power they or their family had. Men and women had some choice in their jobs. For example, some men cooked and some women hunted. Men could also become warriors, or fighters, after going through a special set of **rituals**.

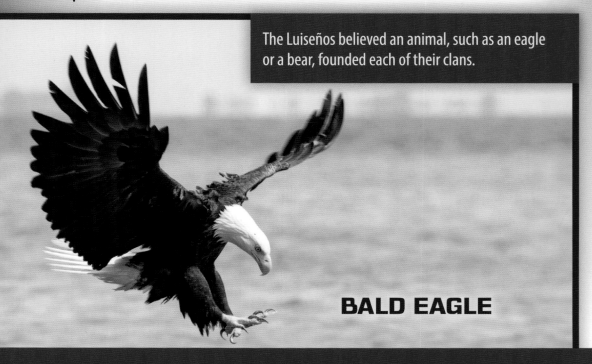

The Luiseños believed an animal, such as an eagle or a bear, founded each of their clans.

BALD EAGLE

BLACK BEAR

The smallest Luiseño social unit was the family. Several families made up a village, and every Luiseño village represented a clan. There were also slaves living in villages. These slaves were children and young women who had been captured from enemy groups.

A chief, who was known as the *nó't*, ruled each Luiseño settlement. Assistants, known as *paxá*, and a council of village elders and religious leaders aided the chiefs. These positions of power were usually handed down from fathers to sons.

CHAPTER SIX

VILLAGES AND CHIEFS

Each Luiseño village maintained its own treaties with other communities. A few senior ruling families in each settlement provided political leadership. These families almost always guided community life.

Each Luiseño village had its own territory where its people had the right to hunt and gather. Lands were divided between individuals, families, and the community as a whole. Outsiders who wanted to come into these areas had to get **permission**. Many of the groups that lived away from the ocean owned smaller areas of the coast where they would go each year to fish, hunt, and gather. The Luiseños carefully marked the different areas of land.

The chief of each village—the *nó't*—had an unusual amount of power over the lives of his people. These men organized and oversaw community work efforts and religious ceremonies. They also served as military leaders during times of war.

The Luiseños cared greatly for their lands and took pride in governing themselves. Leaders made sure all members of their society had food and shelter. They also made sure each individual knew his or her responsibilities.

CHAPTER SEVEN

SPIRITUAL LIVES

The Luiseños had rich spiritual lives. Most of the spiritual leaders were men. They were believed to have special abilities that could be used for both good and evil. They knew many secret rituals, dances, and songs that supposedly had the power to make people well or sick. These people were always respected and sometimes feared.

Luiseño chief Marcus Golsh entertained children with stories in 1959.

The Luiseños believed their ancestors traveled to the sky to escape death. They believed the Milky Way was the home of their spirits.

The Luiseños had dozens of religious ceremonies, which were often filled with dramas and storytelling. Men usually led these ceremonies and performed sacred dances. Women participated by singing and preparing food. There were rituals for every stage in a person's life, including the passage of young men and women into adulthood. Other religious celebrations marked the changing of seasons.

Families and individuals often had their own sets of sacred songs, rituals, and knowledge, which were handed down to their children. These things were rarely shared with other community members or outsiders.

CHAPTER EIGHT

THE LUISEÑOS AT WAR

For the Luiseños, warfare was an important part of life. Conflicts occurred for a variety of reasons, including competition over natural resources, such as fishing and gathering areas. Other struggles developed from accusations of witchcraft or **trespassing**. The Luiseños rarely fought with each other. However, they sometimes fought wars against other nearby peoples, such as the Cahuilla. They were almost always at war with the Kumeyaay villagers to the south.

Luiseño warfare often focused on raids, or surprise attacks. Once a war had begun, groups of young warriors invaded enemy territory and captured or killed anyone they found. Enemy men and women were usually killed, but the younger women and children were taken as slaves. The Luiseños were cruel warriors. They took prisoners, stole items for celebrations, and would destroy whole villages if given the chance.

The Kumeyaay people lived near the Luiseños. Even though they were often at war, the two groups sometimes traded goods.

CHAPTER NINE

EUROPEANS ON THE PACIFIC COAST

During the middle of the 18th century, several European powers fought for control of North America. Spain feared losing California to England or Russia, as this would leave Mexico and Peru open to attack.

In 1769, King Carlos III of Spain sent an expedition to California to set up a colony. The colony would be made up of military bases and missions. Missions were religious communities with the goal of transforming the American Indians into Spanish citizens. A group of priests, headed by Junípero Serra, was selected to establish the missions.

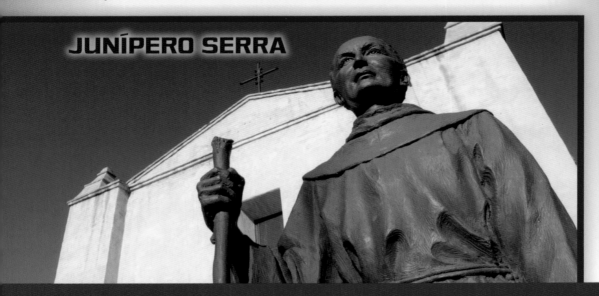

JUNÍPERO SERRA

In 1776, Junípero Serra founded Mission San Juan Capistrano between San Diego and Los Angeles. The Native Americans who lived there—the Acjachemens—were close relatives of the Luiseños.

Missions were gradually established along the Pacific coast. Each settlement served as a church and a kind of government representative. Missionaries hoped to introduce the American Indians to the Spanish way of life, which included a whole range of new ideas, animals, plants, and tools.

CHAPTER TEN

MISSION SAN LUIS REY

In 1795, Spanish leaders established a mission for the Luiseños. In 1798, this mission was named in honor of Saint Louis, or San Luis, a former king of France. Between 1798 and 1832, a priest named Antonio Peyri built a strong relationship with the Luiseños. Everyone at Mission San Luis Rey seemed to understand and respect each other. They shared in the work, the community's products, and its harvests. By the end of the mission era in 1834, there were nearly 3,000 Luiseños at Mission San Luis Rey, making it the largest Christian community in California.

In 1821, Mexican **rebels** won their independence. Spain gave up its claim to California, and the missions became part of the new nation of Mexico. The years that followed were very hard on the Luiseños. They lost many of their rights and much of their property to the newcomers.

Mission life allowed the Luiseños to learn new skills and trades from the Europeans. They built amazing structures, including the main building of Mission San Luis Rey. It was the largest man-made structure in California at the time.

CHAPTER ELEVEN

AFTER THE MISSIONS

The Mexican government ended the mission system in 1834. In 1846, the U.S.-Mexican War began. It ended in 1848 with a treaty that made California a part of the United States. The U.S. government was terrible for the Luiseños. In 1850, the governor of California called for a war of **extermination** on the American Indians.

In 1891, the Act for the Relief of Mission Indians established **reservations** for the remaining Luiseños at La Jolla, Rincon, Pauma, Pechanga, Pala, and Soboba. The new reservation system provided some help, but the Luiseños were still told that their culture, religion, and language were bad or wrong.

By the end of the 19th century, many Luiseños had realized that if they said they were American Indians, their civil rights wouldn't be respected. Instead, many claimed to be Mexican Americans. The government treated Mexicans poorly, but it treated American Indians worse.

Life for the Luiseños became very difficult after the missions closed. Some American Indians, such as this woman, lived on reservations. The Luiseños fought hard to keep their traditions alive.

CHAPTER TWELVE

PRESERVING THEIR CULTURE

It's unclear how many **descendants** of the Luiseño people are alive today. About 1,800 people lived on the reservations in 1990. The Luiseño culture continues to grow and change, and the Luiseños are working hard to preserve their identity as proud American Indians. Though they've faced many setbacks, they continue their fight for civil rights. The Luiseños have an amazing **heritage** and want to preserve their sacred places and objects.

Ancestors of the Luiseños prospered for hundreds of years before Europeans arrived, and the Luiseños continued to live well at Mission San Luis Rey. Unfortunately, repeated invasions of their land left many Luiseños with very little. Today, some Luiseño groups are fighting for the return of parts of their lost homeland. The Luiseños have played an important part in the larger story of California and the United States, and they deserve to be recognized and treated with respect.

GLOSSARY

ancestor (AN-ses-tuhr) Someone in your family who lived long before you.

complex (kahm-PLEKS) Not easy to understand or explain; having many parts.

descendant (dih-SEN-dent) Someone related to a person or group of people who lived at an earlier time.

discrimination (dis-krih-muh-NAY-shun) Treating people unequally based on class, race, or religion.

extermination (ik-stuhr-muh-NAY-shun) The killing of a whole group of animals or people.

heritage (HEHR-uh-tihj) The traditions and beliefs that are part of the history of a group or nation.

mineral (MIH-nuh-ruhl) A natural substance that is formed under the ground.

permission (puhr-MIH-shun) The approval of a person in charge.

rebel (REH-buhl) Someone who fights against authority.

reservation (reh-zuhr-VAY-shun) Land set aside by the government for specific American Indian nations to live on.

ritual (RIH-choo-uhl) A religious ceremony, especially one consisting of a series of actions performed in a certain order.

trespass (TRES-pas) To cross a boundary into someone else's land without permission.

INDEX

PRIMARY SOURCE LIST

Cover
Metates and manos from Mission San Luis Rey, California. Photograph by Nancy Carter. From North Wind Picture Archives, Alamy Stock Photo.

Page 15
Maria Antonia, basket maker at Pala. Photograph by Edward H. Davis. c. 1914. Now kept at the Library of Congress Prints and Photographs Division, Washington, D.C.

Page 23
Kumeyaay people. Illustration by Schott, Sorony, Co., NY. 1857. From Wikimedia Commons.

WEBSITES

Due to the changing nature of Internet links, PowerKids Press has developed an online list of websites related to the subject of this book. This site is updated regularly. Please use this link to access the list: www.powerkidslinks.com/saic/luis